What Do You Want?

Seed
Learning

What do you want?

A hot dog.

I want a hot dog.

What do you want?

A hamburger.

I want
a hamburger.

What do you want?

A donut.

I want a donut.

What do you want?

A burrito.

I want a burrito.

What do you want?

Curry.

I want curry.

What do you want?

Spaghetti.

I want spaghetti.

What do you want?

Fries.

I want fries.

Let's learn more about Saint Patrick's Day.

Color the shamrock.